The
God
Desire

Also by David Baddiel

The God Desire

On Being a Reluctant Atheist

David Baddiel

TLS

TLS Books
An imprint of HarperCollins*Publishers*
1 London Bridge Street
London SE1 9GF

The-TLS.co.uk

HarperCollins*Publishers*
Macken House, 39/40 Mayor Street Upper
Dublin 1, D01 C9W8, Ireland

First published in Great Britain in 2023 by TLS Books

2

A catalogue record for this book is
available from the British Library

ISBN 978-0-00-855028-8

Typeset in Publico Text
Printed and bound in the UK using 100%
renewable electricity at CPI Group (UK) Ltd

Before the Divine Kingdom can be established
in events, it has to be established in the mind,
in the human imagination.
– *Bishop Richard Harries, Thought for the Day,
BBC Radio 4, 4 November 2022*

We cherish the illusion that exalts us
more than a host of baser truths.
– *Alexander Pushkin*

The
God
Desire

I am an insomniac. There are many potential reasons for this, most of them probably physical, but if you're going to be psychoanalytical about it, and look for something in my childhood, I'd say it was to do with death. When I was six, and first became aware of death, my mother, doing her best to soften the blow, said: 'It's like a long sleep from which you never wake up.' I think from that point I never really wanted to go to sleep again.

I remember that first awareness of death well. I remember lying in my bed – the top bunk of a bunk bed, although I had my own room – and praying to Hashem (one of several Hebrew names for God): frantically pleading with Him that my brothers and my mum and dad and my best friend Saul Rosenberg would still be around beyond the grave. That my life as it was in Dollis Hill in 1971 would still somehow continue after death. Which, looking back now, is odd, as Dollis Hill in 1971 was certainly a kind of death.

To be clear, I was not praying to Hashem in the hope of getting into heaven. I went to an Orthodox Jewish primary school, and Judaism doesn't have a clear position on the afterlife. Medieval rabbis did have a conception of *olam ha-ba* (the world to come) but the phrase is not mentioned in the Hebrew Bible. Which is weird when you consider how often Jesus mentions the afterlife. But this is just one of the ways in which Christianity got religion right, compared to Judaism, and went on therefore to completely outclass it in popularity.

Anyway, where my sometime comedy partner Frank Skinner or my wife Morwenna Banks, of Catholic background both, might as children have been praying that they and their family would end up in heaven, rather than hell, I would have been setting my sights lower than that. The idea of post-death neighbourhoods – some nicer than others – would've been very much down the line, as far as I was concerned. I just wanted existence. I just didn't want to die. And I was much, much further from death than I am now.

The God desire

When you write a book, you spend a fair bit of time thinking about the epigraph. In truth, it's probably procrastination. Writing a book is hard, whereas decorating a book – choosing a cover, blurbs, epigrams – is not, comparatively. I chose two quotes which you may have just read. I like those two. They are, I think, apposite.

But the one I really wanted to use was this:

> A close friend once said to me: but don't you
> *want* to believe in God? I said: yes. Desperately.
> That's why I know He doesn't exist.

It's the opening sentence of *The Belief System*, a book by an atheist thinker, Virginia Brook. But Virginia Brook is a character of my own devising, who appears in my own play, *God's Dice*. And using one of my own quotes as an epigraph is just too naff. I thought I might get away with it on the basis that this book is about the non-existence of something, so perhaps it would be apt to begin with a quote from a book that doesn't exist – I thought that might be meta and clever enough to carry it through – but in the end, it's just too Alan Partridge a move.

Nonetheless, the quote does sit at the centre of this polemic. Most arguments for atheism are philosophical.

Sometimes they tie themselves in knots grappling with the issue of how you can prove the non-existence of something. At heart they are based on the idea that there is no evidence for God's existence, therefore He doesn't exist.

Which might seem like atheist job done. But it isn't, as there is no concrete evidence for the existence of, for example, dark matter. Dark matter, which makes up 94 per cent of the bloody universe. No evidence for it at all. It's just a conceit, invented by scientists to explain away the (large) parts of existence that they can't account for. Which is problematic, from a no-God point of view, as that's basically the same conceit that priests and imams and rabbis have always used God for.

My argument, on the other hand, is, in a general sense, psychological. It requires an admission, which frankly most atheists, I've noticed, aren't prepared to make. Which is: I love God. The idea, that is, of Him (for the purposes of this polemic I'm going to stick with the patriarchal, traditional pronoun, although I believe a modern God would almost definitely have a Twitter bio that ended They/Them). Who would not love a superhero dad who chases off death?

Macho atheism

Some non-believers reading this will think: Speak for yourself. It's common among atheists, in trashing religion, also to trash the rewards of religion. Or, to be more specific, to disavow the presence in themselves of what religion is there to serve. There is something a little macho in atheism. Some atheists divine – correctly – that what religion provides for human beings is comfort, and then, in a way that can feel a bit adolescent, they feel impelled to say, essentially, 'Comfort? That's for babies.' But humans, a subset of which includes all atheists, *are* babies, however old and intellectual and cynical they grow. No matter how adult and controlled we seem on the surface, underneath we are a hive of wailing, impulsive, immediate need.

I'm happy to admit to my own babyishness. This may be because – or, rather, why – I am a comedian. Much comedy is just that: stripping away the façade of adulthood. We are all winging adulthood, truly: there is only one adult in the world whose age in his soul lines up with the age he in fact is, and his name is Michael Gove. That's why people laughed (a long time ago, when I virtually was still a child) at a sketch called 'History Today' that I performed with Rob Newman in *The Mary Whitehouse Experience* in which two distinguished old history professors slagged each other off like primary schoolchildren.

I am flawed and shallow and scared and often desperately in need of comfort, both psychological and physical. I am also, however, someone with enough self-awareness to perceive these as urges, rather than as ideas. My thinking self, in other words, is distinct from my urgent one. Not all the time – I often find myself thinking, I must eat NOW or I will die, even when it's only eleven in the morning – but I'm conscious, even as I think it, that this isn't a logical way to understand the world, or even the phenomenon of feeling peckish. I know even as I experience desire that it is desire, and that desire provides no frame for reality. The God Desire should not have to lead to the God Delusion.

Yet the desire is real. For me, it is the very intensity of it which alerts me to the fact of fantasy. The need to imagine that there is an exit door – somewhere through which to escape constantly oncoming Death – is one that I can confidently predict exists within the deep recesses of most humans, and the pressure of that desire has always, and will always, lead to divine projection. People talk a lot about what it means to be human, about what separates us from the animals. Some of that is lyrical – love and empathy and stuff (I personally think it can be pinned down to the fact that we are the only animals who feel shame in defecating) – but whether it *makes* us human or not, we are the only animal that from an early age – six in my case, in Dollis Hill – is aware of the inevitability of death. So it is impossible to look at the repetitive creation of legends, across every culture and throughout history, which in one way or another outsmart death and promise immortality, without concluding that God is a projection of a very fundamental desire within us for it not to be so inevitable.

Storified

It's not just death that makes us want God. He services human psychology in a host of ways, providing several buffers from cold dark reality. Death is at the heart of it – all these other ways spring from death or, rather, our consciousness of it – but God also offers *story*. Humans have a need to organise, to structure, the chaos of existence. They need to feel that life has narrative. Narrative requires satisfactory checks and balances, such as good being rewarded, and evil being punished. God provides all this. He storifies life.

With story comes another God benefit: *meaning*. A sense, on an individual level, that your own narrative has significance: that it matters, in some way. This can only be the case if Someone or Something is taking account of it. Your own narrative extends to your family or village or country (I refer you to the matter of who it is who saves the Queen*). It extends indeed to human-ity as an idea. We are special, and our relationship to the divine confirms that: after all, God made us in His image and the other animals don't get to go to heaven (which frankly if you like cats as much as I do makes it a version of hell anyway). You see this specialness in lots, by the way, of not-conventionally religious, spiritualist thinking. When Russell Brand says, 'You must define yourself . . . in your relationship with a higher entity', the entity concerned may not be God with the beard and robe sitting in judgement in the heavens, but the concept is serving the same need: for there to be a rela-tionship between you and something eternal, something above, something significant, something that gives you meaning.

All of this indicates another benefit we get from God, psychologically, which is – and I'm aware that this isn't a word – *parent-ness*. God the Parent – God the Father and Mother – synchronises all the other benefits. It is parents who, initially, give our lives meaning and allow us to tell stories about ourselves. It is parents – as we know from my mum's misjudged death-as-sleep analogy – who first try to comfort us with ideas that death is somehow not

---

* See Coda.

that bad. It is parents who take account of us. It is parents in whose image we are indeed made.

And of course, we fear our parents. Which is why God can be both loving and angry and capricious – because once you get to these psychic depths, desire will become contorted with anxiety. In the raging primordial soup of the unconscious a constant conflict is played out between anxiety and desire, and this – as in dreams – creates imaginations (which, like dreams, seem real to us in the moment) that can be both blissful and terrifying. God is this: an archetype, a super-projection, of a parent who can be both blissful and terrifying.

At heart, though, God is all about death. The other issues are spin-offs. The organisation of life into story, the ascription to it of meaning, the heart's cry for an eternal parent protector figure, all these wouldn't be so necessary if we never died, or if, like animals, we didn't know we die. Death doesn't create these needs in and of itself. An endpoint itself is not the issue. Oblivion is the issue. Nothingness is the issue.

A story needs an ending. But the way our most popular stories end, generally, implies an afterlife. Romantic comedies tend to end in marriage, because our culture doesn't know how to represent love as an exciting, passionate thing in the mundane reality of everyday co-existence, but also because the assumption at the end of the romance, at the end of *Pride and Prejudice* or *Notting Hill*, is always that these people's lives will carry on. In *Four Quartets*, T. S. Eliot wrote, 'Humankind cannot bear very much reality.' If death portends only oblivion, and if, extrapolating from oblivion, there is therefore no meaning, no story, no protector and no point, then that is the reality that humankind cannot *actually* bear very much of. I say actually because by the time of *Four Quartets*, Eliot had become a high Anglo-Catholic, and his poetry infused by faith, which makes the quote a perfect mirror-image of the way I think things actually are. Eliot meant that humans cannot bear to look directly at the face of God. I believe that humans cannot bear to look directly at the face of death, and so have invented the face of God as a shield.

Which is why the canard 'There are no atheists in foxholes' is not a good argument for the godly ('foxhole' is a stand-in for trenches, or crashing aeroplanes/sinking ships/deathbeds). They – the godly – really think it's a good argument. There is a long history of deathbed conversions or, to be more exact, of the celebration by believers of rumours of deathbed conversions. From Julian the Apostate (anti-Christian Roman Emperor, who in 363 was supposed to have said, 'Thou hast conquered, O Galilean', as he lay dying in battle) through Tom Paine and Voltaire and Darwin, all the way to Christopher Hitchens, the idea of the non-believer recanting at the last is one that has been deeply prized by those who do believe. This works the other way around, as well. Atheists, who in general should not worship, obviously, but who do worship their atheist heroes, feel the need to refute what they consider a slander. After the *New York Observer* repeated, once too often, that Tom Paine had died 'howling and terrified', and, of course, recanting, an atheist called Robert Ingersoll offered the newspaper's editor $1,000 if he could prove it. They couldn't – they eventually conceded, not particularly gracefully, that Paine had died 'a blaspheming infidel'. Similar rows have surrounded the deathbeds of Darwin and Hitchens, and in 2016 the journalist Nick Cohen wrote a piece in the *Guardian* entitled 'Deathbed Conversion? Never. Christopher Hitchens Was Defiant to the Last'.

To my mind, this speaks again of the machismo of atheists and their need to pretend that they are too hard and adult to require nonsense like comfort and hope in the face of death. You, if you're an atheist, might say no, we don't need *illusory* comfort and hope in the face of death, but to my mind, *all* comfort and hope in the face of death is illusory. Death is shit. It's necessary, and often makes more sense than – whatever the Bee Gees might say – staying alive, but that doesn't make it a good option (it being sometimes the least bad option doesn't make it good). As far as I'm concerned, someone telling me at my deathbed that I will live on in their hearts, or that I can be happy, at least, that I was loved – all of this may be *truer* than 'You're going to heaven', but it's still basically illusory. It's still something that people will be saying to try and make themselves feel better about a situation in which they are powerless. I don't want to get too bleak about it all – quite tough, given how this paragraph has gone so far – but I predict that on my deathbed, my loved ones telling me that I will live on in their hearts will just bring home to me the reality that they too will die soon.

I am not being macho. I am not, by calling it illusory, dismissing comfort. I want on my deathbed all the comfort I can get. Which brings us back to the point. 'There are no atheists in foxholes' is not an argument for the existence of God because an atheist who is *not* trying to be macho knows, like any other human being knows, that whatever someone might reach out to in moments of intense pain or terror is irrelevant to the truth. The idea that someone who has spent their whole life disavowing God might pray to Him to save them at the last is an argument for the existence and the power of fear, not of God.*

---

* Fear is often mixed up, by the godly, with God. I notice that if I occasionally poke fun at Christianity on Twitter, someone will respond aggressively with: 'Let's see you mock Islam now, Mr Edgy', or some such goading. He knows, this goader, that I won't do that. Not because I can't see a way to make those jokes, but because I'm frightened of being killed, obviously. But when the Christian goads me like this, it is not a win for Faith, or Christianity. It is rather, using

I have, as I said at the opening of this book, always been much possessed by the idea of death, but for some time I tried to battle it with a kind of self-criticism. In my late teens, I read somewhere that fear of death was narcissistic, a desire to perpetuate the self for ever, and because I was at the time very politicised, it gave me a way of pushing back against my own fear of death, of telling myself that to fear dying was a symptom of the individualist nature of late twentieth-century capitalism. And thus, I shouldn't fear it. Obviously, that didn't last. I was only a couple of years older when I read, in John Updike's memoir *Self-Consciousness*, these words:

> It is the self as the window on the world that we
> can't bear to think of shutting. My mind when I
> was a boy of ten or eleven sent up its silent
> scream at the thought of future aeons – at the

the tyranny of a threat from another religion in service of an insecurity. It demonstrates only a not-very-Christian craving to be able to use fear to bully in the same way.

As a sidebar, I would add that I *have* written jokes about Muslims. I wrote a film called *The Infidel*, which was about a Muslim who discovers he was born a Jew. It stars Omid Djalili and it's readily available on Apple and Amazon. Yes, that was a plug. Anyway. Comedy-wise many more of the jokes are about Jews, but some *are* about Muslims. However, what there isn't are any jokes about Muhammad or the Qur'an. In *The Infidel*, I joke about people, not the sacred: I avoid blasphemy. I'm fully aware that this, too, is because of fear. I am as happy to cop to fear as I am to childlikeness. In fact, it's kind of the same thing.

thought of the cosmic party going on without me. The yearning for an afterlife is the opposite of selfish: it is love and praise of the world that we are privileged, in this complex interval of light, to witness and experience.

At the time, I was just discovering Updike, open-mouthed, unable to believe that anyone could write like this. It spoke to me of me, as a child, crying to God at the point of knowledge. Updike is talking here too of his early childish understanding of the finality of death. I note, as I write this, that at the start when I recalled my own silent screams to God, I said I was praying to Hashem that not just me, but also my mum and dad and brothers and Saul Rosenberg* could somehow hang out together after death. I think I even included our cat, Phomphar.† So for me, Updike is correct. Our sense of reality – at least, our optimum reality, our best life – is social, not solitary. The lust to survive after death is about staying in the world, in society, more than just staying as one self.

---

* His full name was Saul Jacob Rosenberg. I wonder if you can guess his ethnicity.

† So called because my dad thought that was an onomatopoeic rendering of the noise she made when she was purring. It's interesting that that rendering still has something a bit Yiddish about it. Phomphar herself was not Jewish.

Quoting Updike – a Christian all his life – is instructive. My argument for atheism tends to be reflected back at me most often not by other atheists but by those you might call intelligent believers. I have mentioned how my insomnia may or may not have begun when my mother used sleep as an analogy for death. The flip side of that comes in *Self-Consciousness* too:

> The mind cannot fall asleep as long as it watches itself. Only when the mind moves unwatched and becomes absorbed in images that tug it as it were to one side does self-consciousness dissolve and sleep with its healing, brilliantly detailed fictions pour in upon the jittery spirit. Falling asleep is a study in trust. Likewise, religion tries to put us at ease with the world. Being human cannot be borne alone. We need other presences. We need soft night noises – a mother speaking downstairs. We need the little clicks and sighs of a sustaining otherness. We need the gods.

That is right about sleep, and it is right about religion. It raises a central issue, which is that for Updike, and for other religious intellectuals, the core needs that religion serves, the deep comfort it provides, indicate – it seems – that God *must* exist. Updike knows that at some level this is childish – otherwise he would not have used the analogy of a watchful/listening mother downstairs; nor is he a writer who would have been unaware of what four uses of the word 'need' in the second half of that paragraph suggest – but that does not draw him away from the fact of God.

Yet it draws me – who feels viscerally all these needs as well – to the fact of no God.

You can see the same instinct that leads to God in many other areas where humans create a reality from desire. 'Our minds,' says the writer Maria Konnikova, 'are built for stories. We crave them, and, when there aren't ready ones available, we create them. Stories about our origins. Our purpose. The reasons the world is the way it is.' Which is the point I'm making, except it's from a book Konnikova wrote called *The Confidence Game*, about the history and psychology of con-tricks. People want to believe that they are going to make money, or find love, or be cured of disease; so they believe. And they believe these things not just because doing so will make their lives better, but because such endings to their own stories make *sense*, rounding them off in a way that feels satisfying, and as it should be. Conspiracy theory is similar. Actually, conspiracy theory gets even closer to the mechanics of religion: it offers reassurance, but also evil. A necessary evil. Evil allows for a battle between evil and good, and therefore symmetry and story.

Conspiracy theorists are inspired by a desperate hope that the world, that history, is not just a random series of events. Conspiracy provides narrative. Its theorists are deeply comforted by the idea that reality, as they perceive it, is controlled. It doesn't really matter that it's controlled by the bad people. The important thing is that reality is ordered. It is more comforting to imagine that the world is controlled by evil forces than that it is uncontrolled. This also offers the possibility that this control can be overcome by heroes, and that good will triumph in the end.

Of course, conspiracy theory brings with it a host of other religion-like effects, such as a tribe of people who believe the same thing you do, in opposition to most of the world who are not believers, and the sense that you have seen through the trappings of the immediate and obvious world to a deeper truth beneath.

There is a flaw in my argument, obviously. Things you wish for *can* exist. They can come into being. Sometimes you desperately want to have sex, and sex happens. Or food. Or riches. You might be being beaten up in the street, and you cry out for someone to help you, and someone comes.

Wishfulness in and of itself does not prove the non-existence of anything. 'Nothing is as you wish it,' says the dying wife in Thomas Hardy's *The Mayor of Casterbridge*, and she's certainly right much of the time, but not always. So allow me a refinement. Human beings can desire things they don't have but that existentially exist. A man in the desert desperately wishes for water. There is no water. That doesn't mean water doesn't exist, somewhere.

However. The God Desire is an urge for something to exist for which there is no existential proof, and that no one has, in concrete terms, experienced. Let's call that condition invisibility, by which I mean, not just out of sight, but beyond hearing, smell, touch and, indeed, recognition and location by any form of artificial intelligence. Therefore, my equation is:

desire + invisibility = God.

If we desire something that doesn't appear to exist anywhere – which makes that thing different from sex or food or riches or help from others – we collectively will it into being.

Or to put it another way. The man in the desert wishing for water has drunk in the past. He has swum in the past. Other people, hearing about the man in the desert, know, while feeling sorry for him, that water comes out of their taps. Nothing unreal is being willed into existence by that man's desperate desire for water.

Well, maybe one thing. A mirage, of an oasis.

An alcoholic goes up to the Isenheim Altarpiece

I always think – wrongly – that the God-doesn't-exist-because-anything-so-deeply-desired-must-be-a-fantasy argument will impact on believers, and they will see the truth of it. That doesn't happen. I assume any believers reading this haven't had their opinion changed one iota. I'm not sure whether you should be offered your money back though, as I imagine you didn't really want it to be.

The late writer and critic A. A. Gill, for example, who was a Christian, simply laughed when I put this argument to him. He said, 'That's so Jewish – *I want it so it can't be true.*' I don't see how this is particularly Jewish. I suspect it was more that Gill was one of those people who, when talking to someone Jewish, bundles everything that comes out of that person's mouth into their Jewishness. But I guess there might be something Jewish in it, by which I really mean, depressive.

Meanwhile, I asked Gill why he believed. He told me there were various reasons, but it came down to one epiphany. He had once seen the Isenheim Altarpiece, a painting from the Middle Ages by Matthias Grünewald. Gill told me that looking at that altarpiece he felt that Jesus knew him, understood him, spoke to him. He felt a very profound connection to the figure on that cross. It was beyond words, beyond understanding, but he knew it to be real.

The Isenheim Altarpiece is possibly the most extreme image of Christ on the cross in the already crowded field of extreme crucifixion imagery. It was painted to hang in an Antonite monastery, a place that offered care for sufferers of St Anthony's Fire, or ergotism, a common disease at the time that was caused by consumption of a rye parasite in bread. Ergotism makes blood vessels constrict so severely that blood flow ceases completely. Limbs become gangrenous and can auto-amputate. The depiction of Christ's body in the central panel of this altarpiece was designed to connect with those sufferers. It is an image of a man racked with pain, his body jaundiced and covered in strange sores, his hands spread in a rictus of agony.

At the time he saw the painting, Gill was an alcoholic, and a man in pain. He was trying to stop drinking and having terrible withdrawal symptoms. He had the DTs, was shivering all the time, and felt psychologically and physically tortured. Which means he saw himself in that image of Christ. He saw his own life, his pain, amplified and storified and given artistic weight and gravitas by Matthias Grünewald, by this apparently bespoke Jesus.

So therefore, it wasn't real, if by real we mean an event happening objectively, in the external universe, rather than psychosomatically. It was a moment when something deeply desired – in this case, that a man could feel that his pain wasn't pointless, wasn't just horrible, that it had a greater meaning – came into being, in an epiphany, for A. A. Gill. Gill is dead now and given that, as you know, I really don't believe in an afterlife, in which residents of that space can be hurt or angered by things said about them in this life, I therefore feel OK saying: point proved.

Jesus Christ Superstar
and Tony Soprano

In Norman Jewison's film of the musical *Jesus Christ Superstar*, a central theological issue is resolved. In the big eleven o'clock number 'Gethsemane', Jesus asks God, essentially, WTF? He sings about God's omnipresent brain but points out that He's 'far too hot on when and how but not so hot on why'. And then – it's Ted Neeley in the movie, but he's working from a template provided on the musical's original album by Deep Purple's lead singer Ian Gillan – he hits a high note and really goes for it, while asking this, very understandable, question:

'WHY . . . should I die . . . ?'

The answer is provided – unusually, as God doesn't often do answers – during the orchestral instrumental break that follows. A montage plays, of crucifixions: a stunning variety of medieval and Renaissance frescoes and paintings of Jesus on the cross. Which means the answer is either art – you have to die, Son, to create all this great art (which feels a little harsh) – or, more likely: you have to die for the narrative. This death, and the special brutality and pain of it, will make your story, Jesus, the greatest ever told. It will be told again and again and again, in churches, in museums, in books, on something you don't know about yet called film and television, and look how beautiful that telling will be.

JCS has an amazing libretto, written by Tim Rice. It's now not such an original idea, but in 1970 the concept of making Judas' disenchantment with Jesus political – turning the whole thing into a conflict between two zealots, one of whom feels the other has lost their revolutionary way because he's started thinking that he's the Messiah – was an unbelievably radical reworking of the Gospels. I once met Tim and asked if he had imagined Jesus as just that, as a charismatic rebel but not a God. Rice said yes – his notion was that Jesus had gone mad and started to believe his own publicity. In *JCS*, Judas is the voice of reason.

I have no issue with that. As I say, it's a brilliant reboot. But when I watch that musical, I think something else is going on, too. Because Andrew Lloyd Webber's music – which (I don't care how uncool saying this makes me) is very beautiful indeed; perhaps the word might be divine – creates another possibility. It creates the possibility that Jesus *was* the Messiah, which makes that musical, like a lot of great art, ambiguous. Perhaps he was mad, or perhaps, when everything slows down, and a group of (extremely 1970s) dancers sing 'You'll get the power and glory', and over them, Jesus sings this lovely short aria . . .

> Neither you Simon, nor the fifty thousand,
> Nor the Romans, nor the Jews . . .
> Nor doomed Jerusalem itself
> Understand what power is
> Understand what glory is
> Understand at all . . .

. . . perhaps that music is saying, He *was* God.

Anyway. He wasn't. But for me the interesting thing is: I want this ambiguity. I think it makes *Jesus Christ Superstar* a greater work of art, a greater story. And I think I also want it because I want God to exist.

I bring this up because I wonder if my own sense of godlessness is not macho – as I perceive the atheist urge sometimes to be – but masochistic. After all, I find God's non-existence deeply depressing. Why not therefore invent some version of God that works for me? Why not find Him, indeed, in intellectual reworkings like Updike's? I had a conversation about religion on Twitter a while ago with Naomi Alderman, the writer of the Baileys Women's Prize-winning book *The Power*. Alderman comes from an Orthodox Jewish background but left that community some years ago. She agreed that atheism is the only 'sensible position from which to run our courts, our government, our science', but then went on to tweet the following:

Naomi 🔒 @naomialderman · Oct 15 ···

yes. I personally take the Karen Armstrong view which is that religion is another field of human creativity like music, dance, storytelling or sculpture. some people will be moved by and drawn to it, it will leave others cold.

💬 1   🔁   ❤️ 2   ⬆️

Naomi 🔒 @naomialderman · Oct 15 ···

(my mildly cheeky response is to say that it's also an undeniable fact that God does exist in the sense that Tony Soprano or Odysseus or Buffy the Vampire Slayer exists: as a character many people enjoy thinking about and telling stories about)

Alderman is correct about the undeniability of this version of the existence of God. God is clearly an amazing literary character. But I think Alderman is doing something a bit more than that, neatly evinced in her use of the word 'cheeky'. She is not using God's fictionality to confirm His non-existence (even though, in a wider sense, she accepts that). She is using it to blur what existence and non-existence are, by pointing out, cheekily, that fictional characters exist. Tony Soprano exists, and will continue to do so, in a way that James Gandolfini, the actor who played him, now does not. Tony Soprano, created to represent an iconic good-bad father figure at the centre of a version of humanity that is frightening and destructive and disordered, lives long after the death of the physical frame that contained him: he *is* God, more or less. Or at least, one of many versions of Him that exist in art and literature and film.

It's clever, this, drawing on a post-modernist idea (I think: I've never quite known what post-modernism is, but it's got to be this kind of thing) that all reality is a textual construction anyway, and so therefore a character who exists in fiction is as real as one in flesh and blood. Why can't I get behind this, in terms of God? It's a way of thinking about God that might suit me and salve my big old existential despair.

Except it won't. Because one thing I do know about Tony Soprano is that when I die, Tony Soprano will have no more reality for me, because nothing will have any reality for me. So therefore, the God-as-literary-character idea is, as far as the fear and the screaming void go, no *use*. The intellectual post-modern intertextual reworking of God is no good for me. In the fist game of my psyche, this God is paper, and death is scissors.

Be kind!

I've noticed something else about atheism: it's not very fashionable. It had a moment in the early part of this century, when the journalist Gary Wolf coined the term 'New Atheists' to describe a loose collective of writers that included Richard Dawkins, Christopher Hitchens, Dan Dennett and Sam Harris. But by 2015, the *New*

Republic was publishing an article entitled 'Is the New Atheism Dead?' and prominent scientific writers such as David Sloan Wilson and PZ Myers were publicly distancing themselves from the term.

You may spot that over the same period of time, an all-encompassing cultural phenomenon developed. I know that many things have been ascribed to the rise of social media, but the truth is that social media has had an intense effect on how we think and how we discourse, and particularly on *how we judge*. One of the changes that social media has wrought, for all its involvement in drives for social justice, is a new individualism. I say new because it's not, as individualism would tend to be in the past, straightforwardly market-driven. It comes, in fact, from an idea perhaps summarised by the popular hashtag #BeKind. #BeKind is used in all sorts of ways on social media – including by people very much not being kind to those who they are aggressively scolding via the hashtag for a perceived lack of kindness – but it is the culmination of a sense that if everyone has a voice, and, more importantly, an identity, then everyone's voices and identities must be respected. It's relativism, but a much more insistent type than hinted at by the philosophers who might have invented the term centuries ago.

There is some progress here. Social media has disrupted the one-way traffic of ideas from the traditional platforms – politics, the Church, TV, radio, books and so on – to the public. The conversation has become a lot more restless than it was, with much more to-and-fro. Very little can be just straightforwardly handed down from those with a voice to those without one, because everyone, now, has a voice, and everyone can push back. Obviously, social media has devolved into its own hierarchies, favouring those with large followings, but still, there is a sense of a mass voice that lies in wait ready to react to anything that anyone may try to impose on the culture.

But there is a problem, perhaps an insoluble one, that comes with moving away from a traditional structure in which truth is handed down from above to one in which truth can be disputed by everybody, and that problem is this: what happens to the truth? It's complex, because the truth that has historically been handed down from above has been riddled with lies. For centuries the Church handed down religious untruth as truth (and burned people at the stake for deviating from it). Religious authorities in other areas of the world did the same. Kings and queens handed on a different kind of religious untruth, about their divine right to power. In the twentieth century, fascist and communist despots presented to their populations another kind of effectively religious untruth. And, of course, this still goes on.

But throughout this history of untruth, there has also been progress towards something that might be called actual truth, and that is the thing we call science. That too is handed down, because most of us are not scientists and must accept what scientists have figured out, some of which will later be proved to be wrong, by other scientists. But within the multiple grey ontological areas here, there is a core reality: which is that science – even when science itself, with Einstein, took a deep dive into the idea that all things are relative – can provide some objective truths. The earth goes around the sun, is an objective truth. The earth is round, is an objective truth.

Meanwhile, if you'd said to most people twenty years ago that a technology was about to come into being that would allow everyone to share everything – all their personal stories, all their information – you'd have said, possibly, 'Well, that'll increase the sum total of truth in the world.' What you'd have been missing if you'd done that – I'd have done that, at the time – is that people don't tell *the* truth. They tell *their* truth. Which means that a lot of people tell their different truths. Which is why what we have now is a kind of Babel of Truth, in which people can claim, and make other people believe, that the earth is flat.

This has a political component. We saw – and see – a particular type of truth-distortion with Donald Trump, with the anti-vaccine movement, with the growth of various forms of conspiracy theory. A high point was reached in 2017, when the White House spokesperson Kellyanne Conway, in response to a question as to why Trump's press officer had apparently lied, stated that he wasn't lying, he was deploying 'alternative facts'. How we all laughed at that. But that was because it came from power. On social media, other types of alternative facts are presented as truths – personal truths, identity truths, political truths, sometimes a mix of all of these – and those who would laugh at Kellyanne Conway very much demand that these truths, because they come from disempowered voices, be respected. *People should be allowed to live how they choose* is a statement you hear on Twitter and Instagram and TikTok a lot, and of course that is true. But there is a kicker to it, which the purity spirals inspired by social media reach for all the time: *and their version of reality mustn't be questioned*.

I'm not going to do that: heaven forbid. But I do think that somewhere in this new principle of respect, of #BeKind, of not contradicting someone whose truth feels marginalised, is the assumption that the idea of objective truth is itself suspect. That anyone claiming any access to such truth is likely to be shutting down other truths in so doing, and that is, at best, unkind, and at worst, an Old World-centric imposition of White Cis Hetero power and privilege.

This is quite a long way round of saying the following: stating that God doesn't exist, and that this is likely to be an objective truth, is contrary to the modern notion that everyone's individual constructions of reality are equally valid. Because obviously if your construction of reality is that God *does* exist, and made you and your world, it is indeed an unkind shutting down of your identity to have that refuted. This was summed up for me in January 2023 on reading a preview in the *Guardian* of a new Channel 4 sitcom about a family belonging to an apocalyptic church, which commended the show on 'never punching down at religion'. In a moral universe dictated by social media, punching up and punching down are the new markers of good and evil, and if religion is no longer considered a vastly powerful and high-status force, but rather a series of fragile and individual identity-based beliefs that only the unkind would mock, then atheists become pariahs.

In the philosopher Scott Hershovitz's book *Nasty, Brutish, and Short*, he relates discussing the reality of God with his four-year-old son Rex, who says, 'God isn't real . . . But when we pretend, he is.' Which is a deeply profound truth about God. But it is also a truth about how we live now: that our construction of reality slips and blurs, to allow for pretence to become actuality. #BeKind may be behind this, but it is exactly the same unkind process by which in George Orwell's *1984*,

O'Brien holds up four fingers to Winston Smith and tortures him until he sees three. Not until he says he sees three; until he *sees* three.

Leopoldstadt

As ever, with modern social media-driven culture wars, it's about power, or at least, the perception of power. Social media likes to defend the perceived powerless from the perceived powerful, and atheists would be perceived to be wielding the power here. Not least because most well-known atheists are white men who come from a Christian background. This becomes clearer when you note that Richard Dawkins gets much more stick for saying things about Islam than he does about Christianity. There would certainly be an argument that since Dawkins writes from a position against all religion, his beef with Islam should just be filed under that, but it gets read, a lot, as a white man dissing Muslims.

I, of course, come from a Jewish background. But I know that won't protect me from anyone who feels that my atheism is an example of power punching down. As some of you may be aware, it is my opinion that when it comes to claiming any kind of kinship with the power-less, my particular background doesn't count.

On which note. In the summer of 2021, I went to see Tom Stoppard's play *Leopoldstadt*. It's a drama about being Jewish by a Jew who has spent most of his life in denial of – or at least not very interested in – that aspect of his identity.

The opening section of *Leopoldstadt* includes a Seder. The Seder is the meal and prayers event that Jews do at Passover, or Pesach (The Last Supper was almost certainly a Seder). Early in the play, there is a bit where a child asks about the significance of eating parsley – one of the many foodstuffs that you eat before the main meal – and is told that it is a reminder of the bitterness of the time of slavery for Jews in Egypt. That's wrong. Slightly. The parsley, which should be dipped in salt water, represents the tears shed by Jewish slaves in Egypt. A separate ingredient, specifically called bitter herbs, or maror (normally a small slab of horseradish), equates to the more general sense of bitterness.

I wrote to Tom, who I had met not long before going to see the play, to tell him this. It was a side issue, as I really wanted to express how much the end of the play had moved me. *Leopoldstadt* also ends (spoiler alert) with a Seder. During the eight days of Pesach, Jewish households are meant to eat no bread, only unleavened bread, or matzoh (a reference to the biblical story that Jews had to leave Egypt hurriedly and didn't have time to let their bread rise). Several matzoh sit in pride of place on the

Seder table and are eaten throughout the Passover night, but one of them – called the Afikomen – is hidden by the adults. At the end of the meal, the children hunt for it. When they find it, they return it to the table – it's broken into pieces and distributed, and that is the last thing eaten at the Seder – and traditionally the children are given presents in return.

The Seder in the first act of *Leopoldstadt*, set in a Jewish household in Vienna in 1899, is a huge, lavish family affair, with multiple characters. The Seder that ends the play is a flashback, sparked by a reminiscence from one of the only surviving characters – Rosa, who escaped to America. 'I forgot,' she says, 'where I'd hidden the Afikomen.'* As she says it, the characters from the

---

* This is another anomaly, which I didn't write to Tom Stoppard about. He wrote to me about it, when I showed him the manuscript of this book. You may have spotted it. I say in the previous paragraph that the Afikomen is hidden by the adults and the children hunt for it. But Rosa, who is referring to a long-gone past, when she was a child, says 'I forgot where I'd hidden the Afikomen.' Tom told me that this issue was pointed out to him, but only at a time when that line was already landing in the play in a way that felt unchangeable. So on the basis that many people customise their Seders personally, he added a line earlier where the Grandma says 'In this family, the youngest child hides the Afikomen.' I've never heard of a family that does that, but it's not impossible (in my mind, this wouldn't mean the adults hunt for it, which would just be odd, but that the older children do). The interesting thing is that I found the line so powerful that, even given my strange need, despite my atheism, to have all micro-Jewishness present and correct in a drama I'm watching, I didn't even notice this.

original Seder – all dead, all murdered – flood back onto the stage.

Watching the play, this destroyed me. I wept. I sat in my seat as the lights came up, unable to move. I felt, in truth, anger, as other theatregoers, non-Jews, just got up and collected their coats and programmes and left (annoyed, reasonably, that I was blocking their way).

I'm telling you all of this because I want to make it clear – perhaps to myself, because it confuses me at times too – just how Jewish, despite, or rather through, my atheism, I am. Obviously, the powerful effect that the end of *Leopoldstadt* had on me might be nothing to do with religion – it might just be to do with the laying waste and injustice of the Holocaust – but I don't think so. Its effect was surely due to many things *connected* to religion: ritual, language, stories, the poetry and magic of it all, remembering Seders at my childhood house in Dollis Hill, hunting excitedly with my brothers for the Afikomen. So, yes, my reaction was to do with religion – but not God. I didn't feel I needed to tell Tom Stoppard about this tiny error in his play concerning parsley versus horseradish at the Seder because it contravenes strictures handed down by a supernatural being. I felt I needed to tell him because it's something I know because I am Jewish, and it feels very deeply part of me to know it.

* * *

It is notable, I think, that none of the New Atheists come from an ethnic minority background with a religious component. OK, Sam Harris's mum is Jewish (his dad was a Quaker), but I can't work out if he actually – I'm going to use the modern term – *identifies* as Jewish. Some of them did grow up in the Church. Richard Dawkins was an altar boy and it sometimes seems to me that his attitude to religion is in violent reaction to that, an attempt to cough out any last shards of that upbringing from his intellectual throat. I think it is almost impossible to feel this urge if, like me, you're an atheist but also a member of a minority that is associated with religion.

Because, in a way that I'm not sure is entirely graspable to the majority, being in a minority will always be part of your identity. In a TV interview that I did recently with Miriam Margolyes, she talked about her need publicly to condemn the actions of the State of Israel, and about how that urge arises partly from her sense of connection to that country, because she is Jewish. A sense, that is, that she needs to say, 'Not in my name.' I pointed out that when a white Christian man in America goes on a gun rampage, I never see white Christians – even if they may express horror about the atrocity itself – feeling any need to express that horror as white Christians. It would not occur to them, because the shooter's actions, or, say, Putin's, do not, it seems, reflect on them. The majority is felt as a vast sea, whereas minorities are a series of islands, on which all members of each minority are felt to live, and each individual's behaviour threatens the possibility of judgement, a judgement that will be cast on the entire island.

In my writings about antisemitism, I have always made it clear that I believe antisemitism is racism, rather than simply religious intolerance. This is a cornerstone of my argument about what modern antisemitism is.

But I have inserted an adjective there that I don't – and didn't in *Jews Don't Count* – normally apply to the word antisemitism: *modern*. It is arguable that the idea of racial antisemitism only really began in the late nineteenth century, when the word antisemitism was coined by the German journalist Wilhelm Marr, and various fashionable ideas of racial stratification coincided with the theory of eugenics, creating a host of really very bad philosophies and movements. Obviously, it – racial antisemitism, as opposed to religious – became dominant in the twentieth century, culminating in the Holocaust, and similarly I have no doubt that antisemitism is now predominantly racial.

However, sometimes, when I'm talking about the way in which antisemitism is overlooked or demoted in the present high-trigger awareness of discrimination in general, I do say, 'Despite, y'know, two thousand years of persecution.'* So if I was to force myself under my own linguistic microscope, I'd point out that there is a flaw in my argument here, or at least, a bifurcation. Because Jews, you might say, have not been subjected to two thousand years of racial persecution. Most of that time, it would have been religious. Most of it was entirely about them praying to the wrong God.

Or was it, in truth? I played York Opera House in 2021 with my comedy show about trolls (a fair bit of which is about antisemitism). Before the show, I walked, as I have done before, to Clifford's Tower, where in 1190, 150 Jews – fathers, mothers and children – committed suicide rather than convert to Christianity, as a baying mob outside were demanding. The tower was set on fire (the one I was looking at – described, interestingly, as a 'beloved' monument – was built on the same site soon afterwards).

That's religious antisemitism, right? Well. Not exactly. Because a few Jews did decide, rather than die, to go outside and accept conversion.† They were immediately murdered by the mob. Which expresses the same point

---

* The y'know is a fairly typical – I'd say fairly Jewish – bit of undercutting from me, aware that the entire history of Jewish persecution is a large and gravitas-filled reference point, and I'm trying to take some of the air out of sounding like I'm stiffly and grandly reaching for something very heavy and important to make my point.

† I would've been one of those Jews.

I've made before, many times: that I'm an atheist, but the Gestapo would shoot me tomorrow. The issue for the mob was not really that these Jews inside the tower didn't believe in Jesus. The issue was that they were Jews – a race portrayed as devils on every church wall, resented as moneylenders and suspected of the blood libel. I would contend, that is, that Jews have always been positioned as alien and monstrous and vampiric by the various majority cultures they have tried to live within.

Even before the nineteenth century, religious anti-semitism had always contained elements of racial anti-semitism. Which might partly explain why I responded like I did to watching *Leopoldstadt*. I don't believe in God. That perhaps is clear by now. But it is simplistic to imagine that because I don't believe in God, my Jewish identity can be easily excised from Judaism.

I have done jokes that suggest it can. Such as this joke:

> People say to me, how can you be an Atheist Jew? I say: I don't believe in God, I believe in Larry David.

Which means for me Jewishness is about culture, and that includes comedy. But there is an episode of *Curb Your Enthusiasm* in which Larry visits some Orthodox Jews (to get Richard Lewis moved up the waiting list for a kidney transplant – maybe best if you just go and watch it), and while staying in a skiing chalet with them, he eats

41

some traife – unkosher food – and to restore that plate to spiritual cleanliness is told he has to bury it in the garden for three days. Which is so niche-Jewish, even I'd never heard of it. But the point is, the religion hangs around. Being a cultural Jew still involves knowledge of – interacting with, being ironic about, having a comic take on – the religion.

And sometimes, like when I'm watching *Leopoldstadt*, the irony falls away. A friend of mine – a man of science, an atheist – whose son died tragically young, sang Kaddish, the Jewish prayer for the dead, at the funeral. This is what it means in English.

> Magnified and sanctified be Your name, O G-d, throughout the world, which You have created according to Your will.
>
> May Your sovereignty be accepted in our own days, in our lives, and in the life of all the House of Israel, speedily and soon, and let us say, Amen.
>
> May Your great name be blessed for ever and ever. Exalted and honoured, adored and acclaimed be Your name, O Holy One, blessed are You, whose glory transcends all praises, songs and blessings voiced in the world, and let us say, Amen.

The usual stuff of prayer, the endless OCD-like repetition of praise, the desperate hope that if you say something enough times, a fragment might get through the ether. I do not find it moving.

But the Hebrew:

> *Yit-gadal v'yit-kadash sh'may raba b'alma dee-v'ra*
> *che-ru-tay, ve'yam-lich mal-chutay b'chai-yay-chon*
> *uv'yo-may-chon uv-cha-yay d'chol beit Yisrael,*
> *ba-agala u'vitze-man kariv, ve'imru amen.*

Or rather the Hebrew – because the sound in my mind carries the association of the script, of the ancient hiero-glyphic, which, because I had to learn it at my Jewish primary school, I can read:

יִתְגַּדַּל וְיִתְקַדַּשׁ שְׁמֵהּ רַבָּא בְּעָלְמָא דִּי בְרָא כִרְעוּתֵהּ, וְיַמְלִיךְ
מַלְכוּתֵהּ בְּחַיֵּיכוֹן וּבְיוֹמֵיכוֹן וּבְחַיֵּי דְכָל־בֵּית יִשְׂרָאֵל, בַּעֲגָלָא
וּבִזְמַן קָרִיב, וְאִמְרוּ אָמֵן.

You don't have to know what it means. At the burial of a son, those words, just the sound, the ancient music, the sonic pain of them, connects you, the atheist Jew praying, and the atheist Jew listening, with centuries of tradition and suffering and defiance. I know I would do the same in my friend's terrible place.*

It's significant that in trying to express this, I've gone to prayer in the face of tragedy. I would not, I think, go to it for celebration, a wedding, a bar mitzvah. Because I think the thing I'm trying to disentangle here is about survival. I am moved by Jewish survival. I am moved by it comically, when before every dinner that marks every Jewish festival, some guest says 'They tried to kill us, they

---

* The Jewish funeral service prayer book, by the way, includes this bit:

37 FUNERAL SERVICE	
God swallows up death forever,	בִּלַּע הַמָּוֶת לָנֶצַח

God doesn't just defy death. He swallows it up. He makes it disappear in the most visceral way, like a parent sucking a poisonous bite from a child's arm. And he doesn't just swallow it up. He swallows it up forever. There's a panic in that 'forever', perhaps because ordinary swallowing normally involves the swallowed thing re-emerging eventually from another orifice. The God desire is forever insecure, and so forever adding layers to God's power. The addition of the layers implies to me the fragility of the belief underneath, like endless coats of paint over a crack.

failed, let's eat.' And I am moved by it seriously. In Simon Schama's televised history *The Story of the Jews*, he talks about the exile of the Jews from Spain in 1492, and he says this about how the diaspora survived: 'There were some things that could not be taken from the Jews. Their language, their music, their poetry, their richly spiced gorgeous cooking, and above all of course, inside their heads, inside their hearts, inside their little books – inside all the things designed for portability and endurance – their religion.' They survived because of their tenacity, their closed-community systems, their ability to move geographically when they needed to. But the *expression* of their survival was the religion. You hear Jewish survival in the prayers, and you see it in the synagogues. Schama continues:

> So when those ships were loaded with Jews and
> their things in the harbours of Iberia, you might
> well have heard the Shama drifting over the waters.
> Hear O Israel, the Lord our God, the Lord is One.

I watch him saying this and am deeply moved. If I am moved by Jewish survival, I am moved by Judaism. There's no getting round it.

A fundamentalist atheist and a Jew

All this is in the service of trying to detail my version of atheism. I would say that I am – a description that my friend Frank Skinner, a devout Catholic, hates (sorry, Frank) – a fundamentalist atheist. By that I mean, if you pushed me, I would say that I don't *believe* that God doesn't exist, I *know* that He doesn't. I know it like I know that stone is hard.

At the same time, unlike most atheists – and I think this is to do with being Jewish and acknowledging and owning that identity as also fundamental in a way that, I guess, Sam Harris does not – I have a lot of time and respect for religion. Or at least: I am not dismissive of religion. I think, first, that religion is a key part of many people's identity, and in some senses, including for me, it may be inseparable from that identity. This is why people get so angry when (some) atheists dismiss religion. It's particularly problematic when atheists don't grasp how intertwined religion is with ethnicity, which is also a key component of many people's identity, as well as their sense of vulnerability. The atheist in me might think choosing to dress like Charedi Jews is medieval – I absolutely do think that – but the Jew in me is still appalled and wants to defend their right to dress like that when I see footage on social media, as I did recently, of a

Charedi man getting abused on an aeroplane by football fans. I don't mean in a 'I may disagree with what you say but I defend your right to say it' way – I mean, I feel the racism of it. I feel, as a Jew, the communal threat of it, even though it arises from the *religious* way in which this man has chosen to dress.

I also think that it is impossible to understand humanity without religion. This is really one and the same argument for why I believe there is no God. I believe the desire for worship is so hard-wired into humans that dismissing religion as fairy tale shows a lack of intellectual curiosity. Or to put it another way, dismissing fairy tales as fairy tales shows a lack of intellectual curiosity. The legends that humans have created over centuries tell you much about humans.

Divine vibration

When I say that I know God doesn't exist like I know that stone is hard, I know of course that stone is not hard. Stone is only hard as conveyed to me by the sensations in my nerve endings as I bring my hand down on one. What the stone is, in fact, is energy. It's a lot of atoms whizzing about, and most of it is empty space. The hardness of stone is a matter of perception, not objective knowledge.

Earlier I pointed out that 94 per cent of the universe is dark matter, and that we don't really know what that is. Similarly, our senses are only attuned to a limited bandwidth of light and sonic waves, and there are enormous frequencies beyond which we never see or hear. The whole universe, as we image it, is indeed a hologram, of sorts. It's various types of quantum-driven atomic chaos made sense of, organised, for us through our eyes and ears by our brains. We kind of do see through a glass, darkly.

This is a critical argument for some of the more scientifically informed of believers. It runs that since we are peering at the universe through a very narrow vista, it is probable that beyond, on either side, above or below that vista, in the unseen, the unfelt, there exists another plane of reality.

Which there does, of course. My issue is: why would that be God? The fact that we don't know stuff doesn't mean that the stuff we don't know is God. Nor is it (since believers who talk like this tend not to be the type who imagine God as the anthropomorphic Big Guy above the clouds) any kind of guiding principle, or divine one-ness, or spiritual vibration.

For the ancients, God was useful to explain away things they didn't understand: storms, earthquakes, why crops didn't grow, disease. I would say the instinct is the same now that we *do* understand those things. We know what causes them. We don't understand dark matter. We don't understand black holes. We don't understand the large sections of the universe that lie outside the doors of our perception. Instinctively, some people, in the face of that blindness and incomprehension, reach for God. And for me *that* – the fact that we've *always* done it – becomes once again an argument for the unlikeliness of that reality. Once, we didn't understand earthquakes, but now we do. We know they are caused by tectonic plates shifting, not God's anger. At some point we will understand dark matter, and know it's caused by [insert whatever the undiscovered scientific explanation is – perhaps someone in three hundred years' time can pencil this bit in*], and not a divine vibration.

The wonder and the truth

In 280 BC, Aristarchus of Samos realised that stars were suns like ours, only a very long way away, rather than, as most of his contemporaries believed, chinks in the floor of heaven. It is possible, and many do, to think of suns like ours existing all over the universe as wondrous. It is also possible to think of it as somehow mundane, or

---

* If you want to know how possessed I am by death, I find writing that caused me a lot of anxiety.

at least, telling of a universe that reproduces a straight-forward reality all over itself. The idea that stars are chinks in the floor of heaven – that is wondrous. That is beautiful. That imagines a plain above us flooded with intense light. You do not have to think yourself in awe if you believe that. It's not true of course. The many suns thing is true.

One way in which I'm a fundamentalist atheist is that I have no need of wonder. I don't mean in my life – I love wonder there – I mean in my argument for God's non-existence. Because God is so hard-wired into the human psyche, atheists seem to feel the need to replace Him with something. I don't. Even though this is at heart what being an atheist means, some atheists feel that it is too bleak to say *it's all just atoms*, and so they say *it's all just atoms and atoms are magical and wonderful*. Which they are, and I'm not disputing the extraordinary mathematics of nature, but to be honest, to really feel that, you need to understand it. You need to be Brian Cox. Which most of us aren't.

Although I'm not sure that Brian's stance of wonder, as evinced in his many documentaries, has that much to do with his mathematical ability. Really, when he's on TV talking about how beautiful an equation is, or staring at a constellation while the music surges and the word *stardust* is said a lot, I think he's not so much stargazing as strategising. I think he's responding to a need that we all have, including atheists, to make reality not entirely mute, which we can do by turning the cold, dark unfeeling universe into God. We make it dance and be joyful and uplifting. We worship at the Church of Nature.

Don't get me wrong: I think a lot of Nature *is* astonishing. As far as I do understand the maths, which is very little, I see that the intricate patterning of the universe could be described as beautiful. But I suspect the urge in scientist-atheists to make this point a lot, to turn the volume up on Nature's wonder, is because the alternative is too depressing. We need to feel in a relationship with *something*, and if that something is taking our breath away, we feel like we are.

But cathedrals and temples are beautiful, too. They are places of wonder. They are designed to transport. Serious places on serious earths, they are indeed, and they can make the person inside feel touched with that seriousness, like he or she is engaged with the great gravitas of things. When you stand in St Peter's Basilica in Vatican City and look up, the beauty and greatness and time and history in the architecture is being corralled into inspiring our sense of the divine, and it's not really that different when a good science programme goes wide with a drone shot and brings up the goosepimples on the viewer's skin.

As I say, I like wonder. But I am obsessed only with truth, and I think wonder, like God, is a projection. The universe can be seen as beautiful and amazing, and it can also be seen as just lumps of rock floating in space. And maybe the closer truth is the lumps of rock one – maybe the wonder is something we're *bringing* to the lumps of rock. I mean, let's face it: *we're* the only ones feeling the wonder. The lumps of rock certainly aren't, nor are they arranging themselves in beautiful fractals for our benefit. In which case, happy though I am to be moved by the stunning pictures and swelling soundtracks, lumps of rock it is.

Now that we're in the realm of science, I should make it clear that I'm not going to get into some of the well-rehearsed evidence-based God versus no God culs-de-sac. For example:

> 'God didn't create the universe, the Big Bang was the start of the universe.'
>   'Well OK then, clever clogs, what was before the Big Bang?'

. . . and all that. This isn't that type of book, and I'm not the person to argue about that, because I don't understand, despite trying quite hard, how time and space didn't exist before the Big Bang. Well, I kind of do, in a having-read-a-lot-of-popular-science-books way. I understand that the random appearance of energy and time out of a singularity accords with the laws of relativity and quantum mechanics. I just can't *imagine* it. I can't imagine what pre-spacetime looked and felt like. And once I can't imagine something, no amount of explaining it to me with equations, or analogies involving ripples on water, or clocks, or hills being built at the same time as holes are dug, will help.

More importantly, it opens up a discursive space which, not to put too fine a point on it, is a fucking waste of time. Because what existed before the Big Bang goes beyond everyone's, even Brian Cox's, imaginative limits. The very idea of using the word 'exist' to describe that . . . time (that's wrong too, obviously) is wrong. As politicians sometimes say these days to evade giving an answer, the premise of the question is wrong.

Believers – or even agnostics* – will bring it up, because to some extent what they want to do in these arguments is head towards a place where everyone has to say 'We don't know.' Which allows the believers, or the agnostics, to say 'Well, if we don't know, then what we don't know might be God.' To which argument I refer my right honourable reader to the point I made a few paragraphs ago.

Most evidence-based God versus no-God arguments are really, I think, just opportunities for sixth formers –

---

* Don't get me started on agnostics.

and I'm thinking of myself forty years ago now – to broadcast that they have depth. There are many arguments available. Rebecca Newberger Goldstein's novel *36 Arguments for the Existence of God* lists, in an appendix, those thirty-six arguments. They are called things like 'The Argument from the Paucity of Benign Mutations' or 'The Argument from the Fine-Tuning of Physical Constants'. The atheist reflex is to refute the arguments by pointing out their logical flaws. This is pointless. It's pointless on both sides. Those who believe in God should not use logical arguments to support that belief because God exists beyond logic and reason. That's why He's God and that's what faith is. Conversely, those who don't believe in God can use logic and reason to deconstruct those arguments until kingdom come (a religious expression, of course) and it won't change the opinion of those who believe because they can always fall back on the beyond logic and reason thing.

But this is, I notice, an argument that classically flows in only one direction. That is, believers put forward a model of why God exists and atheists refute it. My argument flows the other way. Rather than the atheist, as usual, having to prove that something isn't, it invites instead the *believer* to prove that something isn't: namely, that belief *isn't* a function of desire. If I was going to have a late-night sixth-form conversation with a believer at this stage of my life, I would ask them to prove that their conclusion that God exists *isn't* anything to do with their desire for Him to. The easy way to do this would be for the believer to tell me that they believe that God exists but would prefer him not to. That would be the obverse of me believing that He doesn't, but preferring that he did.

When belief is not optional

What Stephen Hawking said is that nothing created the universe. That before the Big Bang there was nothing, and the laws of gravity and quantum mechanics make it entirely possible for the universe to have arisen from nothing. This nothing is what is hard to imagine of course, as we tend to imagine nothing as the absence of something. But this is a deeper kind of nothing, and relates to the God Desire, because similarly we find it hard to imagine the actual nothingness of death.

To return briefly to my deathbed, I also believe not only that should I pray to God while lying on it this will not be an argument for His existence, but that I will not believe it. I think that all the various atheists who may or may not have recanted on their deathbed out of pain and fear in their soul – obviously they don't have one, but hey – they won't have believed in such redemption even as they were asking for it. It's just a scream in the dark.

To be honest, I don't know if believers really believe it. Maybe suicide bombers – the ones who kill themselves in the hope of being rewarded for their actions after death – maybe they do. But I'm not sure one should put too much stock in the self-awareness of suicide bombers. I think it's possible that what suicide bombers crave, like most people (as social media has revealed), is identity, registered as significance among their peers. Or to put it another way: a suicide bomber does indeed kill themselves for the rewards granted to them in the life after death. A real life after death – not the imaginary one where there are virgins in heaven, but an actual future where their names are venerated by others after their limbs have long since stopped flying through the air.

For many centuries, people must have really believed in God and the afterlife. I often used to think about this as I walked past graveyards. I would – employing the doublethink of death, of death imagined as life – think about how many over the centuries have believed, fixedly and absolutely, in an afterlife, and now lie in their coffins, stumped, as it were, wondering what happened: the deadpan dead.

And yet. Apart from a handful of martyrs, for whom the same psychology applies as for suicide bombers, I am led to wonder about the millions of people throughout history who led their lives not wanting to die. In the time of the plague, as far as I can make out, people did not run and embrace plague victims. Why? If so many of them believed so firmly in the prospect of a heavenly hereafter, why was there still such an aversion to death? I know people would be frightened of pain, but surely if you truly believed in heaven, wouldn't you be OK to go through a bit of suffering to get to the eternal bliss? There's hell, yes, but to be honest, life was fairly shit for most people, and anyway, many believers must have felt that they had led a good, Pearly Gates-opening life. With such potential reward, just waiting round the corner, why, throughout history, throughout literature, is death still fearful?

At a time when belief was not optional, Shakespeare wrote *Measure for Measure*, and I can hear, more beautifully written, obviously, my own thoughts on the matter.

> Ay, but to die, and go we know not where
> To lie in cold obstruction and to rot;
> This sensible warm motion to become
> A kneaded clod . . .

Sensible, by the way, as I'm sure is obvious, is not being used here to mean practical – as in not wearing your coat indoors as otherwise you won't feel the benefit when you go outside. It means possessed of senses: of consciousness. Opposite, that is, to a kneaded clod (of earth). Why

would Shakespeare think this was even a possibility?*
How does an Elizabethan have a sense that, really, death
is oblivion? It's a character speaking, of course, but I can
hear in it something, and that something is terror and
knowledge.

I think the flip side of the God Desire is this, an
instinct which might be called the Oblivion Knowledge.
We do all have this. We all have some sense of what
things were like before we were born, and we all know,
really, that that's what we're going back to. I think every
bishop and imam and rabbi knows this, and that's why
so many pray so fervently. We pray and pray and pray,
to drive out that knowledge. The sure and certain hope
of the resurrection is neither sure nor certain, which is
why both of those adjectives need to be in that sentence,
gravely intoned, propping up desperately the word
hope.†

---

* Shakespeare may, in this speech, be referencing the Roman poet
and philosopher Lucretius, whose work *De Rerum Natura* was
rediscovered in Italy in the fifteenth century. It was widely read in
the Renaissance, not least by Montaigne, and is the first known text
to imagine the world atomically. It also argues against the
immortality of the soul. Nonetheless, such a view was, in general, as
the scholar Brian Cummings puts it, 'unsayable in any Christian
context until the late 17th century'.

† There's so much, for me, in 'sure and certain hope'. It sums up the
doublethink of religion, as does that kid saying 'God isn't real but
when we pretend, he is.' Because of course *hope* can never be sure or
certain. It is the nature of hope to be tentative. Otherwise it is not

On nothingness and jam

Bertrand Russell said, 'I believe that when I die I shall rot, and nothing of my ego shall survive. But I should scorn to shiver with terror at the thought of annihilation.' I also believe that when I die I shall rot and nothing of my ego shall survive. But I totally fucking shiver with terror at the thought of annihilation. This is because I am not as lofty a man as Russell, obviously, but there is a touch in this famous quote of that atheist machismo I mentioned earlier. It's there in the word *scorn*. Which is an expression of contempt and disdain for something. Not, I would suggest, in this context, religion. I would suggest Russell means anyone babyish enough to be terrified by infinite oblivion, which, hey, is like water off a logical positivist's back. On which note, it is of course completely illogical to be frightened of death, because, as I have often heard atheists say, you won't know you're dead. The great thing about oblivion is that you are oblivious to it. Which is true, but not very human. Because, as I said earlier, we can only imagine death from life. When we are thinking about it, we are doing it from the point of view of being alive and,

hope, it is fact, or knowledge. By making the supplication end with the word hope rather than knowledge, whoever wrote that prayer has provided a beautiful (in its humanity, its vulnerability) yet unconscious giveaway of the uncertainty of this sure certainty.

really, life seems a *lot* better. I don't even mean that we can't help but imagine death as life inside the coffin – what Updike terrifyingly calls 'the breathless darkness and the narrow house'. That is our horror film imagination, and although it's horrific, I think one can dispel it. The real horror is oblivion, while we know about it. The real horror is nothing, from the point of view of something.

I feel I may need an upbeat here. It's all got very death-y. OK. Maybe this will half-help.

I was watching the comedian Arthur Smith do his show about Leonard Cohen in Edinburgh once, and he quoted a line that I thought Cohen had written, but it turns out was from the Belgian playwright Maurice Maeterlinck. He said this:

The living are just the dead on holiday.

The reason I'm offering it up as a half-help is that, I guess, if there is one thing that being a fundamentalist atheist should lead you to, it's an intense commitment to *Carpe Diem*. As a child, when I asked my parents for a treat of some sort – nice food, to go to the fair, to stay up late to watch the TV – they would often, after refusing, say: 'Jam Tomorrow.' Meaning stop looking so sulky, you'll get these things at some point. Generally, I didn't, which may of course be why I so firmly disbelieve in God.

Because God is all about Jam Tomorrow. And if you believe that neither Jam nor Tomorrow is ever coming, what you should do is really live for today. It should inspire you to grasp life by the bollocks and shoot for the stars and all that because, y'know: YOLO.* Go out and get that fucking jam, David.

The problem is that, to be honest, knowing this is the only life I get, and that there is no hereafter, hasn't really inspired me to live my life like that. I am too plagued by other anxieties and weaknesses – nothing to do with religion or God – that stop me from YOLO-ing my way through the world. The other problem is that when I heard Arthur Smith say that line I felt completely devastated. I hear it often, in my head, much more often than anything about seizing any days.

The living are just the dead on holiday.

I love holidays. So much so that when I'm on holiday, almost always, by about the second week, the holiday gets overshadowed by the fact that the holiday is about to end.

---

* Editorially, I am being pressed to explain this acronym. I don't want to, as those who know will be bored by the explanation, and it feels a bit Grandpa-ish to do so, although obviously it's already quite Grandpa-ish to use an acronym, however ironically, that kids use, or did, in 2015. Anyway. It's the title of a Bond film. Sort of.

This is why I said half-help. I feel it's gone down to more like a quarter now. Or maybe has not helped at all.

Being a spoilsport

A friend once said to me that he doesn't like atheists 'because they're spoilsports'. I think that's a common attitude. It's a more traditional version of what I was talking about earlier, about how it's now considered reactionary/unkind/an abuse of power to tell someone that their construction of reality may be objectively wrong. Being a spoilsport is more benign, in that the notion itself acknowledges that the spoilsport, though a horrible curmudgeon, is right. Someone who tells children that Father Christmas doesn't exist is a spoilsport.

I have children. I like Christmas, for many reasons, none of them to do with Jesus, so I've gone a long way in my time to fool my children about Santa. I have eaten a quarter of a mince pie and half a carrot and left them on a plate near a fireplace, with a small semi-drunk glass of sherry. I even once briefed a Santa – I mean, a man who was playing him – on my children's likes and dislikes so that when they met him, he knew lots of stuff about them. They were wide-eyed with our old friend, wonder.

I loved that. Because I am not, he said plaintively, perhaps defensively, a spoilsport. I like story and fantasy. I like the idea of children believing in magic. I like the idea of adults believing in it too. Or at least, allowing themselves that doublethink of knowing magic is not true and still hoping for some of it in their lives anyway. A bit like how the lyrics of 'Three Lions' assume from the facts that England are going to lose, but hope they might win after all. I'm perfectly happy with – I like, in fact – magical thinking.

I hope that being an atheist is not like barging into a big cosplay convention of comic fans and shouting, 'What are you doing, you babies?! None of these characters are real!' Humans invest emotionally in story in a very intense way. It matters to them. And they are not unaware of the fact that what they're investing in is fictional, even while they build all sorts of cosmetic realities around it. Cosplaying as Spiderman *is* a version of the God Desire – it is about people wanting a certain type of fictional reality to be really real and so creating a whole series of rituals and confirmations that imply that it is – but meanwhile, no one at the cosplay convention actually thinks Peter Parker exists. It's a type of play, and the human mind is good at play. Religion, for most people, is not that. For most people it's too serious for play.

But to come back to the spoilsport thing – I don't remember ever having to tell either of my kids that Santa wasn't real. They just seemed to work it out when they were a bit older. I have no idea if they were deeply crest-fallen, if they felt the world had spoiled their sport. But I do know that if either of them had still been believing in Santa when they were in, say, their early teens, I would have thought something was wrong. I would've felt forced to present them with the tough love of his non-existence. I might even have had to stop eating the quarter of a mince pie. And I particularly like mince pies.

The consequences of atheism

John Gray's *Seven Types of Atheism* is mainly about the consequences of atheism. It's about the social and moral positions that, say, William Empson or the Marquis de Sade, or Dostoyevsky, or – and Gray is generally a bit scornful about them – the New Atheists might come to, having renounced God. He thinks that to be an atheist you have to have great faith in humanity:

> A free-thinking atheism would begin by
> questioning the prevailing faith in humanity. But
> there is little prospect of contemporary atheists
> giving up their reverence for this phantom.
> Without the faith that they stand at the head of

an advancing species they could hardly go on.
Only by immersing themselves in such nonsense
can they make sense of their lives. Without it,
they face panic and despair.

Interesting though this might be, for me it has no relevance. I am not concerned about the ethics, morality or social order that a universal conversion to atheism might lean into. If a different understanding of human relations is created by atheism, then fine, or if the illusion of God is necessary to sustain a certain altruistic underpinning to society, also fine. But saying 'We have to sustain God because otherwise the social fabric will collapse' or 'All moral precepts stem from some religious background', or, from the other side of the coin, 'We are perfectly capable of organising ourselves ethically without God' – these ideas have nothing to do with the truth, which is that there is no God. I am really in this book only talking about why I think that is a truth. I'm not talking about what follows from that truth. Whatever follows from the truth is what follows. I was once asked to be president of the British Humanist Association and said no, mainly because I thought it might involve a lot of going to speak to no-doubt-wonderful-but-quite-a-long-way-away-from-where-I-live local humanist societies. But it's possible that underneath this was a nagging doubt as to whether I am a humanist. I like humans, and I like the idea that humans should be self-reliant about how humanity works, rather than outsourcing those regulations to a Higher Non-Human Being that doesn't exist, but it's an adjacent point, as far as I'm concerned, to the basic truth of God's non-existence. And actually, if a set of rules claiming to come from an imaginary, superstitious authority turned out to be a good cadre of codes for humanity to live by (as some religious rules are, of course – Thou Shalt Not Kill, for example), I think I'd be fine with living by them, while knowing their provenance was nonsense.

The trouble with the whole discussion about what the prospects might be for humans if God completely exited the stage is you get into a lot of arguments about whether humanity is naturally kind or whether altruism can be baked into us by empathy rather than handed down by moral lessons and . . . y'know. Meh. Atheists throughout the centuries, from Spinoza to Santayana, seem to have felt the need to say, there is no God, then what? And to go on to offer various ways in which humans can still survive adequately or reorganise their thinking, to combat things like 'the problem of evil'. Whereas what seems to me to need to be said is there is no God: that's just what is. What follows from the truth is not the responsibility of the truth. There is no compunction on the part of a fact to mitigate the consequences of the fact. A stone is thrown into a river. It creates ripples. Those ripples may be smooth and beautiful to look at, or they may lead to a boat upending and people drowning. The fact of the stone being thrown remains the same.

I am not uninterested in talking about what might happen to us if universally, across the globe, across all cultures, there was an acceptance of God's non-existence. It could be a fascinating discussion. But in order to say there is no God, I don't feel the need to prove that we can be OK without God. We might not be OK without Him. That indeed might be why we hang on to Him. It makes no difference to the fact of His not being there.

The greatest story ever told – Jesus as hero

The 'problem of evil/pain/bad things in general' is, by the way, another one of those late-night, sixth-form arguments that bedevils this conversation. Atheists who say 'If there is a God, how come there's poverty/bone cancer/Infowars? Eh? Tell me that?' are, frankly, shit atheists. God, clearly, doesn't have to be nice. I mean, He *wasn't* nice, anyway, until Christianity came along – He was either amoral (and tended to have multiple personalities) or, in the Jewish case, mainly cantankerous. The association of God with goodness is a Christian idea, and like many Christian ideas, has proved very successful. It's in tune with what people want. It serves the narrative purpose of religion, as humans prefer stories that reward good over evil, which creates a satisfying order to things – also if God isn't good, it's quite hard to understand why anyone is praying to Him, as He might on a whim just decide to destroy the world anyway.

But if I did believe in God, I would bat away the problem of evil, because God's moral compass would of course be beyond human understanding. What I might say, if I did believe in God, is *you must see God as an artist, a storyteller*, and obviously, in a great story, you have to have evil. Because without evil there is no good. Without villains there are no heroes.

The creation of Jesus as a hero is key to Christian success. Screenwriting manuals will tell you that one of the first things you need to do with your central character – with your hero – is make the audience empathise with them. Or to put it another way: get your hero, early doors, to do something that will make the audience *like* them. This empathy can take many forms. The most famous screenwriting manual, by Blake Snyder, is called *Save the Cat!*, because getting your hero to do that – save a cat – early on in a script is one way to create that empathy. And undeniably, it helps if your hero is relatable: if he is, for example, a man, who lives on earth, rather than, say, a formless mist. It also helps if he comes from a low-status background, if the odds are stacked against him, and if he sacrifices something for a greater good. The story of Jesus is the Greatest Story Ever Told, because two thousand years before *Save the Cat!*, it really hits a lot of the correct commercial storytelling beats.

God cannot fulfil this hero's role. God cannot be low status. Which is why Jesus, the cross-breeding of God and man, is a brilliant conceit – it creates a worship that is also a kind of empathy, a unique combination of adoration and identification. You can see it in the central images that define Christianity, as opposed to its older, considerably less successful parent. Judaism's icon is a star, and not a heavenly body, but a topological representation of a star. It is, like the religion, abstract, mystical, philosophical. Conversely, a man on a cross generates intense empathy. A man on a cross who is there because he's sacrificing himself for your sins is almost the perfect encapsulation of the modern idea of the hero.

Jesus can also kick ass (I'm aware this now sounds like the sort of thing a trying-to-be-cool pastor would say in an American Christian film). This too is important for his heroism – it isn't just passive. In a documentary about the comedian Bill Hicks who died in 1994, his sister said of him: 'Bill wanted to be like Jesus. But Angry Jesus, Jesus throwing the moneylenders out of the temple.' This is what a lot of people on social media want to be. They want to be not just good but *oppositionally* good, angrily overturning injustice in their goodness. That's really very much sexier. Good needs to be activated, by fighting against evil. The New Testament, again, had all these beats down.

In a car with Frank Skinner and his sins

When, in the early 1990s, I first became friendly with Frank Skinner, we were on a long car journey. We'd just done an Amnesty International gig in Manchester and were driving cross-country to Birmingham, where he was dropping me off at New Street Station. The roads were, I remember, extremely foggy. Which added to the intensity of the conversation, much of which was about Frank's spiritual anguish.

His problem was that he couldn't take communion. More specifically, his problem was that he was divorced from his wife, and as the Catholic Church does not recognise divorce, this meant that he was, in its eyes, committing adultery by living with his girlfriend. The problem with *that* was he was therefore unable, in church, to confess and repent his sin – of adultery – and swear never to commit it again. Without this, he couldn't

be granted absolution, and without being granted absolution, he couldn't take communion.

Not being a Catholic, it took me a while to get my head
around the various convoluted steps of this. In my
memory, it took most of the journey. In my memory, in
fact, I'm still trying to work it out at the very end of the
drive, just before I step out of the car, when, having kind
of got the actual nuts and bolts of it under my belt, I
asked the cut-through question:

'Sorry . . . but . . . why are you bothered about this?'

And Frank said: 'You don't understand. I think I will
burn in hellfire because of this.'

Frank was right. I had not understood that. Obviously,
the whole conversation had been about him being a
Catholic, but I had not recognised, not in any visceral way,
what that *meant* for him. This was my own failing. One of
the things about growing up around Orthodox Jews is that
you never quite have to deal with any sense of the reality
of religious belief. Judaism is a religion of codes and acts,
of saying this before you wear that, of eating some stuff
and not others, of 613 Mitzvot. It's like a big, extremely
complex manual. You act out your belief through sticking
to the manual. There is very little in the way of actual
imagination of the supernatural. Which allows for a
strange disconnect between the religion and, well, God.

Quick story to illustrate this. I sometimes get asked,
these days, to be the public Jew at public Jewish events.

This is something which frankly, with the whole donning of the Mr Jew mantle, I've brought on myself. But a lot of the time I don't want to do these events.* I do have one prime excuse up my sleeve, or thought I did, to bat away these requests. Last Chanukah, I got a phone call from my local rabbi. I wasn't even aware that I had a local rabbi. Nonetheless, he'd somehow got hold of my number, and, in the manner of a man very certain of his moral probity, he launched straight in with a request for me to come and light a big menorah that was going to be standing outside the synagogue this year.

I didn't much fancy doing that, so I played my trump card. 'So sorry to tell you this, rabbi,' I said, thinking I'd better break it to him gently, 'but I'm an atheist.'

'So am I!' he said, brightly.

This has now become a story I tell in stand-up, but it illustrates a genuine point beyond the laughter, which is that to be a Jew, even a practising one, you don't have to have much of a sense of God. What you need to have is a sense of ritual.

This meant that as a young man – as a young atheist – I didn't really have to deal with the cognitive disso-nance of having friends who were religious. Since at that point most of my mates were Jewish, I didn't have to

---

* To be honest, a lot of the time I don't want to do *anything*. I just want to stay at home and watch reruns of *Four in a Bed*.

process the idea that some of them might be properly clever and yet deeply believe something I hold to be absurd, because the nature of belief in Judaism doesn't involve anything that concrete in the way of belief. It's more like having to process the idea that some of your friends might be really smart but also have an intense form of OCD, whereby they must light candles at a certain time every Friday night while reciting very specific words.

Becoming friendly with Frank, an extremely bright man who believed a more literal version of his religion, was a challenge. But there is something exciting about that level of cognitive dissonance, about having to accept that here is someone I think of as an intellectual peer, yet a cornerstone of their thinking is diametrically opposed to mine. It's the reverse of the way that social media has forced disagreement to go.

Frank has continued to believe. He has written a great book called *A Comedian's Prayer Book*. It's funny, of course, but it also attempts to deal with some very specific issues that are brought up by believing in God. One chapter is devoted to imagining how in the afterlife Frank might deal with a scenario in which on arriving in heaven he discovers that his mother is in hell. Another discusses the quandary of being someone whose belief gives him a smug certainty that will be proved right, after death, but who then worries about how that one-upmanship will be lost when the truth is revealed to everyone, as it will be in heaven. These are light-hearted dilemmas, but between the lines, Frank is genuinely wrestling with the imaginative contradictions of belief.

He's not alone in this. I read St Augustine's *Confessions* recently. Like Frank's book, it is in part an address to God, and like Frank's book, it has some questions:

> Who will grant me to rest content in you? Why do
> you mean so much to me? Help me to find words
> to explain. Why do I mean so much to you, that
> you should command me to love you?

There are many more. Both *A Comedian's Prayer Book* and Augustine's *Confessions* share a sense of the mystery of the divine. That's common across many religious texts – the idea that God is inexpressible, beyond human understanding. But I'm not sure how easily humanity sits with mystery. I think human beings presented with mystery will dig away at it. That's why we like whodunnits. We want to know the how and the why. We want to know the details. Even if you believe that God, or life after death, is at heart ungraspable to us, it's natural to try and imagine it, and an imagination involves questions. To build a picture of something, you colour it in, you fill in the gaps, and that's where the literality will rush in. That's why Frank Skinner and St Augustine, both of whom believe in the mystery of the divine, end up un-mysteriously wondering what heaven actually looks like, why God did this, or that, and what the whole thing means for them.

The religion of quantum physics

Like a lot of blokes of my age and type, I'm fairly obsessed with quantum physics. My play *God's Dice*, mentioned earlier, was about quantum physics, and religion. In my own case, there is something specific going on, which is that my dad was a scientist who'd managed to lift himself out of poverty in Swansea by studying chemistry, and who when I told him that I was going to study arts subjects at A-level said, it's a waste of a brain. So although I did go on to a career in the wishy-washy world of the arts, his influence has definitely stayed with me through the idea that proper hard thinking, real cerebral work, only really happens in science.*

But also, something non-specific to me, which is I think you get to a certain age, as an atheist, and, like

---

* I'm not sure you need my dad's terrible parenting to leave you with this thought. Most people who work in the arts probably share this insecurity.

everyone else, you do still wonder, even though you know as an atheist that the answer is kind of *nothing*, what's it all about, Alfie? Quantum physics provides a way into that. Because quantum physics, as it drills down into the minutiae of things, seems to be a way of contemplating the universe that isn't airy-fairy. It feels like there's an answer in the microscope, that if you *look* hard enough, the mystery of existence will clarify. It doesn't, of course, because quantum physics, like all science, doesn't answer Why, it answers How. There is no explanation in quantum physics for why a wave function collapses into a particle on observation, just that it does. The explanation will be found in maths, which most of us will not understand, and which provides anyway no whys, only delineates precisely the how.

But that non-understanding calls up, I think, a familiarly religious instinct. There is a big market in popular science books about quantum physics because there is something mystical about the subject. There isn't, in reality – in reality, as I say, it's just maths – but we think there is. Or rather, we have projected mysticism onto that branch of science. It's not a long jump; you can see it in the titles. If you look on Amazon for books like *What Is Real?* by Adam Becker, or *The Hidden Reality* by Brian Greene, or *Something Deeply Hidden* by Sean Carroll, or *Reality Is Not What It Seems* by Carlo Rovelli, they appear on the same search pages as books like *Finding Faith: A*

Search for What Is Real by Brian D. McLaren. Both religious books and quantum physics books play on the notion of the real, on the conviction that actual reality is something that exists beyond our immediate apprehension.

When I read these books – the physics ones, not the religious ones – I get a sense of deferred epiphany. Meaning, a sense, a glimmer, of 'I get it! I finally understand!', which as I read on, always vanishes. As Richard Feynman said, no one really understands quantum physics. Somewhere in the combination of the idea that quantum physics offers the deepest dive available into the way the universe works and the fact that no one really understands it is a servicing of the God Desire.

It's strange, in fact, how much of quantum physics is religious. It offers, for example, in its most popular element, many-worlds theory, a kind of immortality (you may die in this world, but not in thousands of others). The Copenhagen interpretation of quantum mechanics, which includes the already mentioned observer effect,*

---

* The observer effect, to explain it no doubt wrongly, implies that observation and measurement affect the phenomena being observed and measured. Most significantly, a sub-atomic particle, like an electron, is, until the point of measurement, in a superposition; that is, existing in a wave of possibilities, not precisely locatable in space and time, but suddenly, at the point of measurement, it is. What is human-centred about this is the notion that somehow or other we have an effect on reality. Significantly, I would say, we have an ordering effect on reality. Reality is chaos, until we notice it. I suggest that in the past we invented God as our measuring instrument for similar reasons.

completely centres human experience in the workings of the universe, much like religion did in the days when it insisted the sun and stars went round the earth. The interpretation includes awe-inspiring phenomena, such as what Einstein called 'spooky action at a distance', where two previously paired particles can somehow instantaneously transmit information – or at least, be connected – to each other, even if they are situated light years apart.

I know quantum physics is servicing a religious urge because I got excited when I heard about spooky action. This was because, as I've perhaps now exhaustively explained, I'd like God to exist. By which I mean, what I'd like to exist are magic and miracles, and this seems a kind of miracle. It is actually true that in the quantum world things happen which are sort of miraculous. There is a sense in which this branch of physics has elaborated a reality that in its grains, its tiny building blocks, is a vibration of infinite possibility, and once you're using phrases like vibration of infinite possibility, you're getting quite close to what a lot of people say when they describe themselves as not-traditional believers but think there's got to be some kind of something out there somewhere.

The many-worlds theory, by the way, has, I've noticed, been very taken up by cinema and TV. Superhero films endlessly flit in and out of the multiverse. I like these films, but worry that they are basically a short cut, writing-wise. If in every story, everything is possible, narrative discipline becomes irrelevant. The whole point of fiction, the difficulty of it, is choosing which narrative path to take at key points in the story, and if all of these are available at all times (and are reversible) then the choosing of them has no real consequence, and story is consequence. In *Everything Everywhere All at Once*, a 2022 film that got great reviews (it is extremely enjoyable), a Chinese-American middle-aged woman moves between multiple lives and personas in an infinity of genres, lives, deaths and possibility. But in the end – spoiler alert – what she needs to sort out for the film to finish are simple issues to do with her life in this life. Which is a religious narrative. There are heavens, there is magic, there are miracles, but they are only available if you're a good person in this life. And something else, which is there are heavens, there is magic, there are miracles, but we can only see them through a glass, darkly (I'm aware I've used that phrase already, but we're talking now about everything, everywhere, all at once) – they fly like visions across our apprehension, but *really*, reality is here. The multiverse, in our popular imagination of it, does the religious cake-and-eat-it-thing, of implying the existence of fantastical worlds beyond our imagination but still centring this one, here, the one we actually live in, as the important one in which we are judged.

That phrase 'the one we actually live in' is important. Relativism, even scientific relativism, can be frustrating. There may indeed be many universes, in the same way that there may be many realities, and politically and socially, many truths, but sometimes you do want to say, yeah, I accept all that, but actually, you know what, stone *is* hard. However much the words *stone*, *is* and *hard* are concepts, and the thing we call a stone is in fact a fizzing fractal of atomic energy held with enormous internal atomic magnetism in a single mass which creates a nervous reaction that the brain interprets as intense pain when that mass is thrown against your soft skull, sometimes you want to say that all you're doing by insisting on that as the *real* truth is making the expression of how things are take longer. And almost definitely by the time you've said all that, you'll have been knocked out when you could've ducked.

My point being: it is true that our apprehension of the world is a construction – a story, in fact – to allow our brains to make sense of it. But that construction for the most part, is as true as we are going to get. Our consciousness may storify but that story is still our reality, and the reality is that that consciousness will shut down, at which point that story will end. That actual magic may be going on in the tiny chains of the universe makes no difference. I may not know whether stone is or isn't objectively hard but I do know that I will not be able to debate that after

I'm dead. The universe may be infinite, but consciousness – the consciousness that science tells us somehow acts on the universe – is not. Quantum physics excites me because it offers the real possibility of a world beyond, but focus on it for any length of time and, like a particle you cannot locate, it vanishes.

What about the animals?

Is it worth arguing the case for atheism? Surely, as time, with science and progress, moves forward, belief declines anyway? Surely, really, having a go at God is just shooting a pretty big fish in a barrel?

Well, not exactly. Overall, it is true that, when polled, fewer people believe in God than they did fifty years ago. But still, globally, more believe than don't. In America, although the figure used to be higher, over 80 per cent of citizens still say they believe in God. Which would suggest that, whatever the evidence, a large proportion of humanity is always going to put some sort of faith in the divine.

Also, statistics aside, any sense – among rationalists – that religion's time as a key force in world events has passed has been proved wrong – by 9/11, by ISIS and by the rise of Christian fundamentalism in America. Soon after the war in Ukraine began, Patriarch Kirill, the leader of the Russian Orthodox Church in Moscow, and a close ally of Vladimir Putin, blessed the invasion (although obviously he didn't call it that), saying that its ultimate purpose 'does not have a physical meaning but a metaphysical meaning' and that the course of it will decide 'which side of humanity God will be on'. For Putin – dreaming of restoring the Holy Russian Empire of old – the war is at least part Orthodox Crusade.

It's remarkable how much religion won't let go of history. On the other side of geopolitics, at the time of writing, America was in the grip of a huge culture war about abortion. Abortion, as an issue, could simply be a difference of opinion about where life begins. But it isn't that, really. It is overwhelmingly the case that support for anti-abortion – or, to use their own preferred term, pro-life – movements is religiously inspired. I saw it online on the day that the US Supreme Court overturned the landmark *Roe v. Wade* ruling, when the top trending term on Twitter was not the words 'Supreme Court' or 'Roe v. Wade' or even 'abortion' but 'Praise God'. Almost every account that supported the Supreme Court's decision took that moment as a victory not – or not so much – for unborn babies, but for Christ.

There's another, less topical and more eternal, way in which how we live now is underpinned by a religious belief. I said earlier that what distinguishes us from the animals is that we are the only species who feels shame about defecating (although I have seen dogs that do look a bit embarrassed, at least if they become aware that you're looking at them). It is worth questioning why we feel shame about this. Or rather, why religion, and other moralistic strictures, focus so much on the bodily functions associated with shame. The obvious answer, as regards sex, is pleasure – religion has always been down on physical pleasure because religion tends towards ascetism, and ascetism is associated with some notion of higher thinking or being. But there may be another answer, which would explain why shitting and pissing, which are not straightforwardly associated with pleasure, also invoke shame: along with sex, they are the activities that most remind us that we are animals.

Some religious ideas may be on the decline, but not, I would say, human exceptionalism. Fewer people might believe in God than they used to, yet, although veganism is on the rise, most of us are still perfectly happy with the fact that we kill and eat huge amounts of animals when we don't really need to. Most of us don't bother with questioning this much. But I assume, if asked why we all think it's OK to kill animals and not humans for meat, most would agree that humans are more important, more sacred, more valuable, more entitled to life than animals. There is secular backing for this idea – we have culture and language, and animals don't (not true, they just have different culture and language) – but at heart it's a hangover from religion. It's a hangover from the notion that God made us in His image, and thus we sit at the top of the tree of life.

Martin Amis once said, of death, that 'after forty, it's a full-time job looking the other way'. I sometimes wonder if, at any adult age, it's also a full-time job – although a less conscious one – looking the other way from the killing of animals. I consider most statements on the internet and elsewhere of people claiming to be on *the right side of history* as always specious, but if you are foolishly going to try and imagine the moral order of the future, the one thing I'd be happy to put a small bet on is that in three hundred years' time people will see our industrial slaughter of animals as a type of genocide.

Because another thing we look away from, in the killing of animals, is just how much they are like us. One of the things the internet has done is circulate, on a vast scale, short films of animals being cute. A lot of the time this means: being like us. I watched, once, some YouTube footage of a pig who had been raised by a specific human and allowed to grow old. In the clip the pig sees this human again after several years of separation and rushes over to the edge of the pigsty, braying and trying to leap the fence with what seemed to my eyes like joy: like the joy of recognition – indeed, of love. If you post links to such films approvingly, cynics – men (always men) born with the knowledge that they know best – will tell you, with lordly condescension, that you are *anthropomorphising*. By which they mean projecting human emotions and responses onto animals. When they say this, they tend not to consider the possibility that if this were not anthropomorphism – if the pig just, as the film clearly suggests, had empathy and memory and other-directedness, if it was really overjoyed to see the person who reared it again years later, if it was capable of love – if the pig were showing the big emotions which we humans think make us special, then complacently slaughtering and eating pigs might become a bit problematic.

But also, the cynic may have to accept something else. That he, as a human, is not exceptional. He might have to accept that perhaps, when you look at how animals, certainly mammals, behave – how they have sex with their genitals, and shit from their anuses, and eat with their mouths – and how they appear, with their noses and ears and eyes and feet and hands/paws – that we are just one branch of multiple DNA outcomes. And accepting that – properly, viscerally accepting it – may not just throw a spanner in the works of complacently eating hot dogs. It also must mean that there is no God. Not least because clearly, coming back to the fact of that ongoing genocide, God does not care about the animals.

Love and the ending

It is traditional in a book like this, which is mainly bleak, to finish on an up note. After all, who wants to close a book which concludes that basically we're all going to die and there's no point to life and yes, The End. I can't see the commercial possibilities there. Unfortunately, this is non-fiction, which means I am bound to the truth. And the truth hurts. We can't handle the truth. Humankind cannot bear very much reality.

It's a problem. I've ruled out wonder at Nature. I've ruled out humanism. I've ruled out the enigmatic magic of quantum physics.

What's left?

I mentioned love earlier. It's often the recourse. Love is often the way, when we search for an ending, a light in the darkness.

Well. I like love. I love my wife and my family. In my head, as regards my people, I have a constant, blind emotional 'please let them be OK' instinct, which is probably as close as I'm going to get to prayer, at least since I was six. But unfortunately, I'm also a bit suspicious of love. At least of its iconic, impersonal state. I'm suspicious of anything that we invest in en masse to define who we are – that lifts us up, that symbolises goodness, and that triumphs, if you believe in it enough, over everything terrible in life – because it sets off my God radar. Meaning: God, in His old various incarnations, is still around, and hasn't gone away, but we have also, where necessary, replaced Him with Love. Which is why I've now capitalised it. I mean Love the deity, as opposed to love, the everyday thing you have with your loved ones. That is real. Love, however, is a construction.

Consider: all the songs, all the stories, used to be about God. Now they are about Love. Not just romantic Love, but Love between family, or Love between tribes, or Love between humanity. Our villains, our Satans, are those who cannot Love, or who put obstacles in the way of Love. I said earlier that romantic comedies tend to end with weddings because there is not enough story, not enough movie, in what comes next: the plateau of ongoing marriage. I believe that to be correct, but it could be refined. If you consider Love, like God, to be something sought after and worshipped, providing the main point of life, then you need a sacrament. You need a point that operates for Love like going to heaven does for God. You need an apex, a wedding, where the story ends and beyond which is just the vague imagination of eternal bliss.

Love makes us feel connected to something larger, better and more significant than ourselves. It makes us feel in touch with angels. When we talk about Loving someone, we say we will do it for ever: it promises immortality. It also, incidentally, separates us from the animals, who we imagine don't experience it.

Love is probably a better thing to worship and to use as a template for positivity than God, but then again, like any deity, it can easily be appropriated and misused. It is not for nothing that the last sentence of *1984* sees Winston Smith feeling, like an epiphany, like the clouds have parted, that he loves Big Brother.

So. I'm running out of ideas. I apologise. I wish I had more.

I guess . . . laughter. That's about it. We do have one thing which actually does separate us from the animals, and it is the ability to be funny (although I've seen footage of chimps apparently pissing themselves at poo-throwing, so I could be wrong again there). Which means we can laugh. We can laugh at our own futility, at nothingness, at the knowledge that the living are just the dead on holiday. I mean that phrase itself is funny. It sends bad shivers down my increasingly decrepit spine, but it is also, at some level, funny.

It's all I got. Sleep well.

Coda

'We're ALL, in a way, in a long queue
on the way to a coffin.'
Lucy Prebble

Earlier in this book, assuming you haven't skipped to the end, you'll have read the sentence 'I refer you to the matter of who it is who saves the Queen.' I was in the process of doing a final redraft of the manuscript when that last word was rendered out of date. But then, living through the days immediately following the death of Elizabeth II, I decided to keep it, because they seemed – as I was experiencing them at the time of writing – instructive.

The phrase 'God Save the Queen' implies of course that God and the Queen are two different entities. But it feels to me now that they are inseparable. By which I mean, she was being revered, on her death, like a deity. She was also deified when alive, obviously. It's remarkable, with its crowns and gold and thrones and capitalisations and special words and kneeling and everything else, how equivalent to God-worship monarchical deification is.

But with her death I noticed an added element.

The keynote of the tributes – beyond all the stuff about duty and public service, and the endless projection about what a lovely woman she was with such a great sense of humour – was longevity. I read again and again words marvelling at the time, the apparently endless stretch of it through which the Queen had been around. There seemed to be a sense that the length of her reign was in itself a mark of something superhuman. In *The Atlantic*, the writer Tom McTague began a long eulogy by saying that 'Longevity alone places her in the pantheon of the royal greats.' A tweet went viral saying that she had reigned for almost one third of the lifespan of America. Another piece by Helen Lewis noted: 'She was six weeks older than Marilyn Monroe, three years older than Anne Frank, nine years older than Elvis Presley – all figures of the unreachable past.'

This points to something, as I would say they are not figures of the unreachable past. The figures of the *unreachable* past are the billions of dead whose names we do not know. Marilyn Monroe, Anne Frank and Elvis Presley are reachable, in our imaginations, in books, in films: they are people whose fame is so great that they are, in the consciousness of the living, immortal.

They too, therefore, are gods, of a sort.* But because they all died when they were young, their immortality took a while to bed in. The cultural presence of the very famous dead builds over time, as their brand deepens, even as their bodies decay. But with the Queen, it seems as if the immortality was, as it were, ready to go; as if at the point of death, her incredibly lengthy life-in-the-spotlight was simply folded into her eternality, a bit like when prisoners who have already served a certain amount of time in prison are allowed to consider that part of their sentence.

One of the most striking things, for a British person, was the era-shifting moment of hearing, immediately after her death, the words – prayer-words, in themselves aiming towards immortality – 'God Save the King' and/or 'Long Live the King'. I'm not sure whether I knew this – I had thought that the new monarch wouldn't officially be the new monarch until the coronation – but in fact Prince Charles became His Majesty King Charles III at the very instant of Elizabeth II's death. This suggests something else about the monarchy that serves the God Desire, which is resurrection. The mystical immediate

---

* We treat objects touched by these people like relics. Frank Skinner, as we know a man of a religious cast of mind, once bought a shirt that had possibly been worn by Elvis at a gig in 1958, for a lot of money. He then later did a documentary trying to prove whether the shirt had really been worn by Elvis, deciding, in the end, to believe it either way, to put faith above evidence.

movement of the throne from monarch to monarch is partly about power but also about creating a sense, a comforting sense, that the institution triumphs over death, and that the soul, the essence, the character at the heart of this story, never dies. It's similar in that respect to another version of God, which is Doctor Who.

At heart, of course, the Queen – despite all the people on my television telling me with astonishing confidence what she was like – was a blank canvas, on which people could project whatever they needed her to be. Primarily, people wanted her to be what I notice the BBC website described her as underneath one of the many films about her life and reign on there: a reassuring constant. There was a queue, which was being live-streamed on the television, four or five miles long, along the banks of the Thames, of mourners waiting patiently to see the Queen's coffin. When they got there, many bowed or kneeled to the gilded wooden box. Often, I noticed though, the queue was referred to as being people there 'to see the Queen' – rather than her body or coffin. As if, that is, she were still alive. It is possible that the queue was as long as it was because those in it, like many others, wanted to feel they had met the Queen, and her deadness needn't get in the way of that. In some ways, her deadness made her royal function – being, as I say, an object on which to project our desires, one of which might be wanting to feel you have been in her presence – easier.

Many of these mourners, when asked on TV what the Queen meant to them, said: she was always there. She suggested, in other words, the possibility of for ever. So that's why I kept the line in this book as who saves the Queen, because it doesn't really matter whether there is a Queen or a King or Emperor or Dear Leader on the throne. They are all another version of God, another phantasm conjured up to combat our mutual fear of nothingness, another story we've bought into that promises that somewhere, there is immortality. One of the things about the God Desire is that it is never quite satisfied – maybe because at heart the collective unconscious knows that God X is not real, so will always move on, in sure and certain hope, to God Y, and God Z. There was another point in this book that you will have read, again if you didn't skip over that bit, where I (perhaps panicking about the point of writing it) spent a while defending the concept of a polemic in support of atheism, because some might think that no one really believes in God any more. But what the Queen's death made clear to me is that I am not talking here just about the religious God. I am talking about the God Desire, about the collective expression, very much ongoing, that results from a need for *something* to be greater than ourselves.

Humanity keeps finding those somethings, keeps investing in them, keeps the myriad worship flames burning. As I get older, I notice more and more of these gods all around me, infinite salves for the same desire, and it hardens my sure and certain sense of the oblivion that getting older portends. The more, that is, it is clear to me how fervent and desperate the God Desire is – how it will, if it needs to, for the reassurance of constancy, inspire hundreds of thousands of people to wait in line for days and nights to bow to a dead body – the more I know, in my reluctant atheist heart, that there is nothing there.

Acknowledgements

I'd like to thank, for their help in the creation of this book, David Roth-Ey, Myles Archibald, Roz Dineen, Iain Hunt, Katherine Patrick, Emma Pidsley, Georgia Garrett and Jonathan Safran Foer.

Also from TLS Books

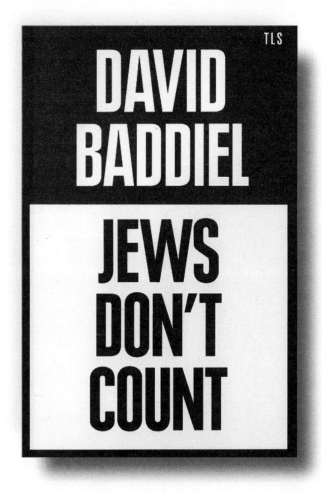

How identity politics failed one particular identity.

'The whole book is just brilliant -
and very much needed'
Simon Schama